Up in
Space

Asteroids,
Comets
and
Meteors

Rosalind Mist

QED Publishing

Editor: Lauren Taylor
Designer: Melissa Alaverdy
Educational consultants:
    Heather Adamson
    and Jillian Harker

Copyright © QED Publishing, 2013

First published in the UK
by QED Publishing,
A Quarto Group Company
6 Blundell Street
London N7 9BH

www.qed-publishing.co.uk

ISBN 978 1 78171 210 8

Printed in China

A catalogue record for this book is
available from the British Library.

Words in **bold** appear in the glossary
on page 24.

Contents

The Solar System

The **Solar System** is the **Sun** and all the things that go around it. This means **planets** and their **moons**. It also means comets, asteroids and **meteors**.

Neptune

Uranus

Saturn

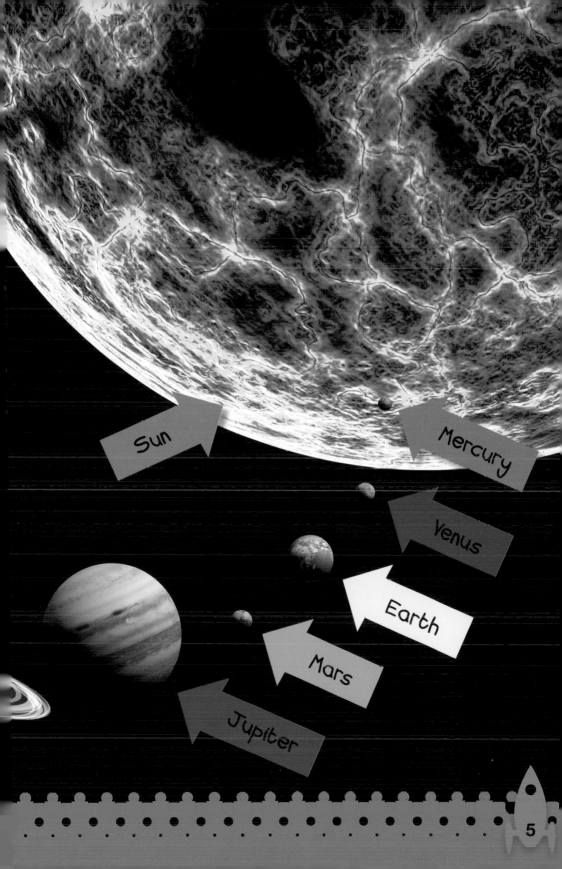

Sun

Mercury

Venus

Earth

Mars

Jupiter

Asteroids

Asteroids are large
chunks of rock or metal.
They move around the
Sun. Planets are
round like a
ball. Asteroids
are much smaller.

Asteroids can be lots of different shapes.

Size and Shape

Asteroids are not usually round like planets. Some can be bigger than a city. Others are the size of a bus.

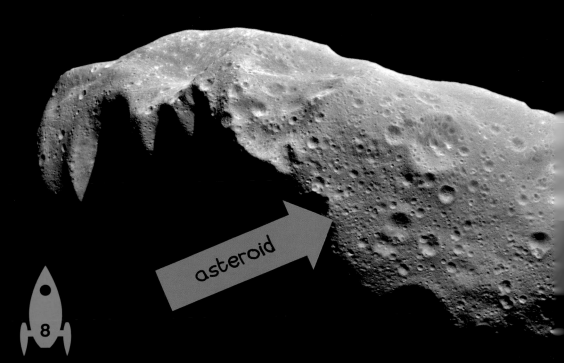

asteroid

Earth

The asteroid Kleopatra is strange. It is shaped like a dog's bone.

The Asteroid Belt

There are lots of asteroids in the Solar System. Most of them are found in groups. There is a band of asteroids between Mars and Jupiter. It is called the Asteroid Belt. It has millions of asteroids.

Comets

A comet is made of dust, ice and bits of rock. As the comet gets closer to the Sun, it starts to melt.

dust and gas

Dust and gas trail from the comet. This is called the comet's tail.

Comet Hale-Bopp

One of the best-known comets is Hale-Bopp. It flew past Earth in 1995 and 1996.

Earth

People could see
Comet Hale-Bopp
in the sky for over
a year.

Ida and Dactyl

The asteroid Ida has its own moon. It is called Dactyl.

Ida

Dactyl is a small moon.
It is about as long
as 15 football
fields.

Dactyl

Meteors

Meteors are small bits of rock and metal. Sometimes they enter the gases surrounding the Earth.

We can see meteors in the sky.

Meteor showers

The Earth can pass near the tail of a comet. Then we see more meteors than usual.

Glowing sparks cut across the sky. This is called a meteor shower.

Meteorites

A large meteor might not all burn up in the **atmosphere**. If it hits the ground, it is called a **meteorite**.

meteor

Earth

Some meteorites are rocks that were knocked off Mars.

meteorite

Glossary

asteroids – small rocky objects that move around the Sun

atmosphere – the gases that surround a planet

comet – a chunk of ice and dirt that moves around the Sun in a long path

meteor – a piece of space rock that forms a streak of light as it burns up in the Earth's atmophere

meteorite – a piece of space rock that falls to the Earth

moon – a natural object that moves around a planet

planet – one of the eight large objects circling the Sun

Solar System – the Sun and all of the things that move around it

Sun – the star that the Earth and the planets move around